DOG PALS

Crabtree Publishing Company
www.crabtreebooks.com
1-800-387-7650

Published in Canada
Crabtree Publishing
616 Welland Avenue
St. Catharines, ON
L2M 5V6

Published in the United States
Crabtree Publishing
PMB 59051
350 Fifth Ave, 59th Floor
New York, NY 10118

Published in 2018 by CRABTREE PUBLISHING COMPANY.

First published in 2017 by Wayland
Copyright © Hodder and Stoughton, 2017

Author: Pat Jacobs

Editor: Elizabeth Brent

Project coordinator: Kathy Middleton

Editor: Petrice Custance

Cover and Interior Design: Dynamo

Proofreader: Wendy Scavuzzo

Prepress technician: Samara Parent

Print and production coordinator: Margaret Amy Salter

Photographs:
iStock: p1 GlobalP; p2 David Baileys, AVAVA, EpicStockMedia; p3 Alona Rjabceva; p4 PakHong, Eric Isselée; p5 Eric Isselée; p6 oxilixo, belchonock, Vitaly Shabalyn, Eric Isselée; p7 Yulia Remezova, borojoint, Vitaly Shabalyn, GlobalP; p8 cynoclub, belchonock, GlobalP; p9 GlobalP, Hongqi Zhang, damedeeso; p10 adogslifephoto, WilleeCole; p11 cynoclub, sale123, Ever, PongMoji, LuapVision, Uros Petrovic, JennayHitesman, Jevtic; p12 Wavebreakmedia, &#169 Lisa Turay; p13 WilleeCole, ncn18, WilleeCole; p14 GlobalP, Chalabala; p15 HannamariaH, Jen Grantham, Eric Isselée, RuslanOmega; p16 pyotr021, IuriiSokolov, Jeanne9; p17 fotoedu, Anna-av, cynoclub; p18 LuckyBusiness, vetkit; p19 Marco Lavagnini, mrgao, cosmln, bina01, GlobalP; p20 adogslifephoto; p21 Wavebreakmedia, mythja, cynoclub; p22 IvonneW, adogslifephoto; p23 cynoclub; p24 Halfpoint, francisgonsa; p25 adogslifephoto, Dorottya_Mathe; p26 Devin_Pavel, Ljupco, damedeeso; p27 glebus, arda savaşcıoğulları, knowlesgallery; p28 GlobalP, nickpo; p29 GlobalP; p32 fongleon356; Front cover: GlobalP; Back cover: Stephanie Zieber

Printed in the USA/072017/CG20170524

Library and Archives Canada Cataloguing in Publication

Jacobs, Pat, author
    Dog pals / Pat Jacobs.

(Pet pals)
Includes index.
Issued in print and electronic formats.
ISBN 978-0-7787-3551-9 (hardcover).--
ISBN 978-0-7787-3580-9 (softcover).--
ISBN 978-1-4271-1945-2 (HTML)

    1. Dogs--Juvenile literature. 2. Dogs--Behavior--Juvenile literature. I. Title.

SF426.5.J34 2017   j636.7   C2017-902515-5
                                        C2017-902516-3

Library of Congress Cataloging-in-Publication Data

Names: Jacobs, Pat, author.
Title: Dog pals / Pat Jacobs.
Description: New York, New York : Crabtree Publishing, 2018. |
    Series: Pet pals | Audience: Age 7-10. | Audience: Grade K to 3.
    | Includes index.
Identifiers: LCCN 2017016736 (print) | LCCN 2017027433 (ebook)
    ISBN 9781427119452 (Electronic HTML) |
    ISBN 9780778735519 (reinforced library binding) |
    ISBN 9780778735809 (pbk.)
Subjects: LCSH: Dogs--Juvenile literature.
Classification: LCC SF426.5 (ebook) | LCC SF426.5 .J35 2018 (print)
    | DDC 636.7--dc23
LC record available at https://lccn.loc.gov/2017016736

CONTENTS

Your dog from head to tail   **4**

All shapes and sizes   **6**

Choosing your dog   **8**

In the doghouse   **10**

Getting to know you   **12**

Doggy diets   **14**

Day-to-day care   **16**

Health and safety   **18**

Dog behavior   **20**

Communication   **22**

Training   **24**

Fun and games   **26**

Dog quiz   **28**

Quiz answers   **30**

Learning more   **31**

Glossary & Index   **32**

YOUR DOG
FROM HEAD TO TAIL

Dogs **evolved** from an ancient **breed** of wolf and were probably the first animals to be **tamed**. They started living with people more than 15,000 years ago. Dogs gave humans early warnings of intruders, and helped hunters by sniffing out and chasing **prey**.

Claws: Strong, blunt claws grip the ground as the dog runs. They are also used for digging.

Tail: The tail gives a good clue as to how a dog is feeling.

Feet: Dogs only have sweat **glands** in their paws, so they have to cool down by panting.

Legs: Powerful leg muscles allow dogs to run long distances.

Eyes: Dogs cannot see as many colors as we can, but they have better vision in dim light.

Brain: The part of a dog's brain devoted to smelling is 40 times larger than that of a human's.

Ears: A dog can hear a sound four times farther away than a human can. They can also hear high sounds that we cannot.

Nose: Dogs have an incredible sense of smell. There are up to 300 million **scent receptors** in a dog's nose, compared to about 6 million in a human nose. Dogs also have a special scent **organ** in the roof of their mouth that aids smelling.

Whiskers: These long hairs around a dog's snout detect air movement and warn of obstacles in the dark.

Mouth: Sharp teeth and strong jaws help with attacking prey and tearing at food.

DOG FACTS

- Bloodhounds can track a human scent over great distances. In 1954, a bloodhound found a missing family by following a trail that was 12 days old.

- Dogs may take 300–400 breaths per minute when they're panting to cool off.

ALL SHAPES AND SIZES

Dogs vary in size and shape more than any other pet. Big or small, long-distance runner or couch potato, **purebred** pup or **mixed-breed**, there will be a dog out there that's just right for you. Here are just a few of the many popular breeds.

Cocker Spaniels were bred for hunting birds. They are eager to please, playful, and active – and they usually get along well with other pets.

Dachshunds were bred with short legs to hunt badgers and other burrowing animals. They like to bark and can be mischievous.

Greyhounds are sprinters and don't need huge amounts of exercise – in fact, they spend a lot of time sleeping. They are bred to chase prey, so need to be kept on a leash when out for walks.

Dalmatians were bred to run alongside carriages, so they need plenty of exercise. They are intelligent but need careful training.

Newfoundlands are strong swimmers thanks to their webbed feet. They are hard-working dogs that once pulled nets for fishermen.

Yorkshire Terriers are little dogs with big personalities. They love to play, but they may bite if small children are too rough with them.

Great Danes are gentle giants. Their sweet nature makes them perfect pets, but their huge size means they won't fit into every home.

Labradors are friendly and intelligent. They need a lot of exercise and are easily bored. They love food and can become overweight.

GREAT AND SMALL

- One of the smallest-known adult dogs was a Yorkshire Terrier that was 3.7 inches (9.5 cm) long and weighed only 4 ounces (113 grams).

- One of the largest-known dogs was an English Mastiff that weighed in at 343 pounds (155.6 kg) and was 98 inches (250 cm) from nose to tail.

CHOOSING YOUR DOG

Before you choose a dog, think about all the things you'd like to do with your new pet. Dogs have been bred to do all sorts of jobs, and this affects the way they behave. Some are clever and want lots of attention, others love to run and need plenty of exercise.

PUPPY ADULT DOG?

If your family is happy to put up with chewed-up shoes and **potty training** in exchange for hours of fun, then a puppy is right for you. Otherwise, there are many older dogs looking for new homes, and they will probably already be **neutered** or **spayed** and potty trained.

PUREBRED  MIXED-BREED?

If you get a purebred puppy, you'll know what to expect when it grows up, but a tiny mixed-breed pup may become a massive adult. Dogs come in all sizes, so ask about the puppy's parents so you have an idea of how big your dog is likely to grow.

LARGE **OR** SMALL?

Think about the space in your home and imagine a large dog there. Would you still have room to move around? Most large dogs need more exercise than smaller breeds, and they cost more to feed. Smaller breeds usually live longer than big dogs.

MALE **OR** FEMALE?

There is little difference between male and female dogs. Males are sometimes larger, while females often grow up more quickly than males and can often start training at a younger age.

WALK TIME!

Be realistic about the amount of time you can spend walking your dog. Don't choose a breed that needs longer walks than you have time for. Surprisingly, a Great Dane needs about the same amount of walking as a Jack Russell Terrier, so size isn't always a guide.

IN THE DOGHOUSE

Puppies are always getting into mischief! You'll need to puppy-proof your home so it's safe for your new family member.

A dog crate will keep your pet safe when you're out of the room, and it's a place for your puppy to rest when it needs a break. A crate that fits in the car will be useful when you take your pet on trips or to see the vet.

To comfort your new puppy, try bringing home some of the bedding from its previous home.

PET CHECK ☑

Does your dog have:

- somewhere cozy to sleep?
- food and water bowls?
- toys?

A waterproof mattress makes a comfortable bed.

PET TALK

I may be happier on your lap in the back of the car than inside a carrier on the journey home.

Puppies are champion chewers, so get some chew toys to save your shoes from sharp teeth.

You'll need a collar, a leash, and an ID tag before you go on your first walk with your furry friend.

STOCK UP ON SUPPLIES

It's best to offer your new dog the same food it is already used to eating. If you want to switch to another food, do it gradually by replacing a little of the original food at a time. You'll need ceramic or stainless steel bowls for food and water, and some treats for training.

A grooming brush will help keep your dog's coat in good condition, and grooming can help to build a bond between you and your pet.

GETTING TO KNOW YOU

WELCOME HOME

Show your pet its sleeping area and then let it explore its new surroundings. Dogs like company, so make sure your pup gets plenty of attention. If you have a crate, keep it close to the center of family life.

Bring your dog home at a quiet time, and don't leave it alone for long periods during the first few weeks. It's good to introduce your pet to people, but give your new friend a few days to settle in before inviting visitors over.

BEDTIME

Dogs normally sleep with their **pack**, so your pup will probably want to spend the first night with one of the family. If you don't want your dog sleeping in the bedroom, a hot water bottle and a ticking clock wrapped in a blanket placed in its bed may help to reassure it.

RULES RULE

Dogs love routines, so set one up as soon as your dog comes home. It will feel more secure if it knows the house rules from the start. Other family members must stick to them, too, so agree on a list before your new pet arrives.

PET TALK

Please don't squeeze me. Dogs don't like being held tightly and I may bite you.

MEETING OTHER PETS

Shut other pets in a separate room when your dog first comes home. When you introduce them, keep one animal on a leash, in a crate, or behind a barrier so they can get used to one another without any risk. Make sure your pets have become good friends before leaving them alone together.

DOGGY DIETS

Dogs are happy to eat the same food every day, and sudden switches can cause stomach upsets. Don't disturb your dog while it's eating and never feed it from the table – your dog wouldn't like you to take its food so don't let it share yours.

FEEDING PUPPIES

Puppies need four meals a day at eight weeks old, and three meals a day between 12 weeks and six months old because they are growing so fast.

FEEDING DOGS

Adult dogs need two meals a day. Meaty dog food is closest to their natural diet and it has everything they need to stay healthy. Dogs should always have a bowl of fresh water nearby, but clear away any leftover food.

Dry food is useful if you have to leave it out during the day.

I'll eat anything, so please make sure I can't reach food that might make me sick.

These human foods are dangerous for dogs:

- chocolate
- grapes, raisins, and sultanas
- onions, garlic, and chives
- pecans, walnuts, and macadamia nuts
- avocados
- salt and some artificial sweeteners
- coffee and alcoholic drinks

TREATS

If you reward your dog with treats during training, give it less food at the next meal. Treats should be no bigger than your fingernail.

PLUMP POOCHES

Wild dogs are **scavengers** and eat anything they find, even if they're not hungry. Pet dogs are the same, so it's important to keep food out of reach. Overweight pets have a lot of health problems, so don't give in to those pleading puppy eyes!

DAY-TO-DAY CARE

Help to make sure your dog stays healthy by keeping a look out for any unusual behavior or signs that your pet might be in pain.
If a dog stops eating, that's usually a clue that something is wrong.

GROOMING

Dogs don't do much to keep themselves clean and some do their best to get dirty. Grooming your pet regularly keeps its coat and skin in good condition.

It may be good for me to have a bath and get my teeth cleaned, but that doesn't mean I have to like it!

BATHING

Dogs are quite happy to be dirty and stinky, so they'll do their best to avoid a bath. You can help to make it fun for them with toys and treats. Use lukewarm water and dog shampoo, and don't get water on your dog's face or in its ears. Be prepared to get wet!

NAIL CLIPPING

A dog's nails need to be clipped at least once a month, or it could suffer a lot of pain – just like you would if you never cut your toenails! Remind an adult when it's time for a trim.

DOGGY DENTAL CARE

By brushing your dog's teeth a few times a week, you can stop your pet suffering painful tooth and gum problems. Let your dog lick some dog toothpaste from your finger and touch its teeth with a soft brush, so it gets used to the idea.

HEALTH AND SAFETY

Pet dogs should be **vaccinated** and neutered or spayed. Your dog should also have a **microchip** to help you identify your pet in case it gets lost.

NEUTER/SPAY

Puppies are spayed or neutered when they are about six months old. This helps protect them from certain diseases. It also makes a happier homelife with your pet, as unneutered male dogs are more likely to fight and **scent-mark** their **territory**.

Microchips are inserted under the skin between a dog's shoulder blades.

PET CHECK ☑

Has your dog been:
- vaccinated?
- neutered or spayed?
- microchipped?

THE GREAT OUTDOORS

Puppies shouldn't go outdoors for walks until two weeks after their final vaccinations, but they still need to learn about the outside world. Try taking your puppy out in a dog carrier, or on a car journey, so it can get used to outdoor sounds and smells.

FLEA

TICK

UNWANTED GUESTS

Keep an eye out for fleas and ticks when you groom your dog. They make life miserable for your pet and can cause diseases. There are injections and treatments to get rid of them, so ask your vet for advice.

WEIGHT CHECK

Being overweight is one of the biggest risks to a dog's health. Extra weight affects a dog's heart and joints, as well as its breathing. Here's how to make sure your pet is a healthy weight:

- You should be able to feel your dog's bones beneath a thin layer of fat.

- Your dog should have a narrower waist behind the ribs.

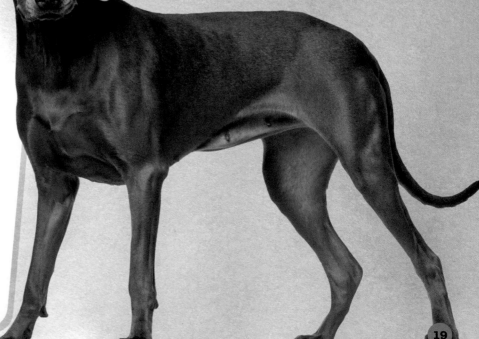

DOG BEHAVIOR

Dogs are pack animals, which means they want to feel part of the group. This is why dogs get along so well with other animals in the house, and especially humans.

BE THE BOSS

Dogs like to know what is expected of them. Discipline and routine help them feel safe and happy. It is important that your dog knows who is in charge and what the house rules are. Be firm with your dog but always loving. If you punish your dog, it will learn to fear you. That will not lead to a happy homelife.

CAN YOU DIG IT?

Dogs love to dig. They also love to bury things! This is a natural **instinct** for dogs. In the wild, dogs used to hunt food and bury it to eat later. With training and patience, you can work to cut down on this behavior.

SHOW ME THE LOVE

Dogs crave affection. They want to know you love them. Some dogs may like to be hugged, but some may not like it. Pay attention to your dog's behavior. If you are hugging your dog and it tries to pull away, try just petting it or rubbing its ears instead.

SEEING THROUGH THE NOSE

Dogs "see" the world through their noses. Their sense of smell is so good they can build a picture with a quick sniff. They will know where you have been, what you have touched, who you met, and what you had for lunch!

PET TALK

If you let me know how you want me to behave, I'll do my best to please you.

COMMUNICATION

Have you ever seen your dog tilt its head to the side while you're talking to it? It seems as though it is listening to you—and it's very cute! Your dog is probably just reading your **body language** though, because that's the main way that dogs communicate.

TAIL TALK

Dogs wag their tails when they're happy, but a wagging tail can also have other meanings:

- A tail that wags so hard it makes the dog's bottom wiggle means the dog is feeling friendly and ready to play.

- A wagging tail accompanied by barking and a long, hard stare means the dog is frustrated, so you should move away.

- If a dog yawns or licks its lips when it's not tired or hungry, it may be feeling anxious, even though it may also be wagging its tail.

- A tail held high and wagging slowly means a dog is waiting to see what will happen.

- If your dog is holding its tail low or between its legs, that means it is feeling nervous.

BE WARNED

An angry dog will have a stiff, upright body and its hair may stand on end to make it look bigger. Its ears will be back, it will bare its teeth, and it may give a threatening growl. This is your warning that it's time to leave quietly and give the dog a chance to calm down, otherwise you may get bitten.

PLEASED TO MEET YOU

When humans meet, they walk straight up to one another and look each other in the eye. Dogs would think this is very rude. Dogs approach each other side to side and sniff each other's bottoms, which tells them all they need to know about the other dog. Imagine if humans behaved like that!

PET TALK

If I crouch down with my bottom in the air, that means I'm ready to play!

TRAINING

Start training your puppy as soon as possible. Training should be fun, so don't let your dog get bored. Short training sessions of less than 10 minutes are best. Never punish your dog because it will be afraid of you and less likely to do what you ask.

GOOD DOG!

Dogs want to please, so they should be given a lot of praise for doing the right thing. Small tasty treats are a good reward when you first start training, but once your dog has learned what to do, your praise should be enough.

SIT!

ROLL OVER!

TEACHING COMMANDS

Start by teaching your dog to sit. This is a good way to keep your dog safe and stop it from running away or jumping up at people.

- Make sure that your dog is concentrating on you.

- Show that you have a treat in your hand.

- Slowly move the treat over your pet's head and say, "Sit!"

- Your dog should move into the sit position as it tries to reach the treat.

- Hand over the treat and give your dog plenty of praise.

- Repeat this, saying, "Sit!" each time.

- Hand signals help your dog to understand.

Once your dog has mastered this, you can teach other commands, such as "Stay!" "Come!" "Down!" and "Roll over!" Always use the same word and tone of voice.

HOW TO POTTY TRAIN

- Take your puppy outside first thing in the morning, and then every hour.
- Give your dog a treat and praise when it goes potty outside. Pick up any mess.
- Never punish a dog for having an accident.

PET TALK

Please teach me only one command at a time—and I would love to play with a toy after training!

FUN AND GAMES

Dogs like different types of games, depending on their breed and personality. Here are some games that you and your dog can both enjoy. See which ones your pet likes best!

TUG-OF-WAR

Most dogs love to play tug-of-war with their owners, but only do this with a dog that isn't stronger than you. There are many different toys designed for this sort of game.

HIDE-AND-SEEK

You can combine a hide-and-seek game with training your dog to stay and come. Try hiding in another room and calling your dog.

POUNCING GAMES

This sort of game is popular with small dogs that have been bred to hunt prey. Tie a toy or an old stuffed sock to a piece of string and pull it along the floor.

MAKE YOUR OWN TOYS

- Put a treat inside a plastic bottle without a lid, or inside a cereal box, and let your dog get it out.

- Braid old T-shirts together to make a tug-of-war toy.

- Tie a tennis ball inside an old T-shirt to make a tossing toy.

CHASE AND CATCH

Some breeds love to chase and catch balls, and a ball launcher will help you to throw the ball even farther. You can play this game with a frisbee and other toys, too.

RULES OF PLAY

- Don't play wrestling games with your dog – you might get hurt.

- Play with different toys and games so your dog doesn't get bored.

- Put toys away after playing.

- Play in short bursts and stop while your dog is still having fun.

DOG QUIZ

By now you should know a lot about dogs!

Test your knowledge by answering these questions:

1 **How does a dog tell you it wants to play?**

   a. It rolls over
   b. It crouches with its bottom in the air
   c. It puts its ears back

2 **Why were Dachshunds bred with short legs?**

   a. So they couldn't run away
   b. To stop them climbing on the furniture
   c. To hunt badgers

3 **Which of these dog breeds is famous for its sense of smell?**

   a. Yorkshire terrier
   b. Greyhound
   c. Bloodhound

4 **Which breed of dog has webbed feet?**

   a. Newfoundland
   b. Dalmatian
   c. Labrador

5 **How many meals should an adult dog have each day?**

   a. 2
   b. 3
   c. 4

6 Which animals did dogs evolve from?

    a. Foxes

    b. Wolves

    c. Hyenas

7 Why do dogs pant?

    a. Because they're hungry

    b. To cool down

    c. As a warning that they may bite

8 How often should your dog's nails be trimmed?

    a. Every day

    b. Every week

    c. Every month

9 Which of these foods is harmful to dogs?

    a. Grapes

    b. Carrot

    c. Coconut

10 How may a dog be feeling if it is yawning when it's not tired?

    a. Happy

    b. Relaxed

    c. Anxious

QUIZ ANSWERS

1 How does a dog tell you it wants to play?

b. It crouches with its bottom in the air

2 Why were Dachshunds bred with short legs?

c. To hunt badgers

3 Which of these dog breeds is famous for its sense of smell?

c. Bloodhound

4 Which breed of dog has webbed feet?

a. Newfoundland

5 How many meals should an adult dog have each day?

a. 2

6 Which animals did dogs evolve from?

b. Wolves

7 Why do dogs pant?

b. To cool down

8 How often should your dog's nails be trimmed?

c. Every month

9 Which of these foods is harmful to dogs?

a. Grapes

10 How may a dog be feeling if it is yawning when it's not tired?

c. Anxious

LEARNING MORE

BOOKS

Baines, Becky. *National Geographic Kids Everything Dogs: All the Canine Facts, Photos, and Fun You Can Get Your Paws On!* National Geographic Children's Books, 2012.

Kalman, Bobbie, and Hannelore Sotzek. *What is a Dog?* Crabtree Publishing, 2000.

Sjonger, Rebecca, and Bobbie Kalman. *Puppies*. Crabtree Publishing, 2004.

WEBSITES

www.lovethatpet.com/dogs/
This website is full of helpful information about dog care. It even has funny pictures of dogs that will make you laugh out loud!

http://pbskids.org/itsmylife/family/pets/article7.html
Check out this site for fun pet facts and great tips on caring for your pet pal.

www.loveyourdog.com
Visit this site for ideas on cool tricks to teach your dog, as well as fun videos, tips, and advice on how to be the best pal to your dog.

GLOSSARY

body language Communicating through gestures and body movements

breed A group of animals with the same ancestors and characteristics

evolve To slowly develop or change over generations

gland An organ that makes fluids and chemicals, such as saliva, tears, and scent

instinct Natural behavior that is automatic and not learned

microchip A tiny electronic device inserted under an animal's skin to help keep track of the animal in case it gets lost

mixed-breed A dog that has parents from two or more different breeds

neuter An operation that stops male animals from being able to make babies

organ A part of a person, plant, or animal that performs a special function

pack A group of animals that live and hunt together in the wild

potty training Teaching an animal to relieve itself in the correct place

prey An animal that is hunted and killed by other animals

purebred A dog that has two parents from the same breed

scavenger A creature that eats the flesh of animals that have died

scent-mark When an animal releases an odor or substance, such as urine, to mark their territory

scent receptors Cells inside the nose that absorb smells and send information to the brain

spay An operation that stops female animals from being able to have babies

tame To make an animal gentle and obedient

territory An area an animal has claimed for itself and defends against intruders

vaccinate To inject with substances that protects humans and animals against serious diseases

INDEX

Bathing 17
Behavior 20–21, 22, 23
Bloodhounds 5
Brain 5
Breeds 6–7, 31

Chewing 11
Claws 4, 17
Cocker Spaniels 6
Collars 11
Communication 22–23
Crates 10, 12, 31

Dachshunds 6
Dalmatians 6
Diet 14–15

Ears 5, 17, 21, 23
English Mastiff 7
Eyes 5

Feeding 11, 14–15
Feet 4
Female dogs 9
Fleas 19, 31

Games 26–27
Great Danes 7, 9
Greyhounds 6
Grooming 11, 16

Health 15, 18–19
Hearing 5

Jack Russell Terriers 9

Labradors 7
Legs 4

Male dogs 9
Microchipping 18, 31

Mixed-breed dogs 8, 31
Mouths 5

Nail clipping 17
Neutering 9, 18, 31
Newfoundlands 7
Noses 5, 21

Other pets 13

Panting 5
Playing 26–27
Potty training 8, 25
Puppies 8, 10, 14

Safety 18–19
Scent-marking 18, 31
Sense of smell 5, 21, 31
Sleeping 12

Tails 4, 22
Teeth 5, 17
Ticks 19, 31
Toys 11, 26–27
Training 13, 15, 20–21, 24–25

Vaccinations 18, 31
Vision 5

Walking 9, 19
Weight 15, 19
Whiskers 5

Yorkshire Terriers 7

NOV 1 9 2018